Steps to Get Out of Poverty

The Hero's Journey

Hattie Spiritweaver

ISBN:1514232685
ISBN-13:9781514232682

CONTENTS

ACKNOWLEDGMENTS

There are many people to thank on this awesome journey called life. I've had many great mentors and met various people along the way who contributed to my path of success.

Each one of them played a role and part in encouraging me to become my best authentic self. I appreciate every one of you, and there are too many to account around the globe. You all know who you are, and whether it was big or small I am grateful for each and every one of you. Now it's time to pay it forward.

1 CHAPTER

POVERTY

Poverty is a journey many people face across the globe. No one wants to be in poverty. No one desires to struggle financially. The question now is what do you do when you're in the trenches of poverty?

You can find yourself hopeless or take responsibility for the outcome of your life.

Depression sets in for many in poverty. The way out of poverty can be a huge challenge, takes inner strength, courage, determination, drive, and a heart willing to do whatever it takes to overcome every obstacle.

What pulls down people, is the negative feedback they receive from society. Poverty is one of the toughest lessons for anyone to learn in society. A huge amount of patience is necessary with self, and other people. A life can never be rebuilt overnight.

Prejudice and discrimination is obvious when looking for a job, in interviews, and even with family members. When people give up on you in society, they see you differently than those who are successful.

Other people don't have the patience, and are impatient with you, because from their point of view all they are looking at is the past, not what you're doing right now. Human nature has a way of dwelling on the past, looking backwards, instead of moving forwards.

The mindset of those around you can be very negative, and have a cause and effect about how you feel about yourself, and the world around you.

When you're in poverty people turn their cheek, write you off as a loser, and have the impression you will never amount to anything in life.

One thing to keep in mind, never allow other people to define you, or write your future for you. They have no idea what your future holds. Never allow them to project their negative point of view on your life.

You may find yourself in a homeless or domestic shelter. There is no safety or security in poverty. There are no guarantees day to day what will happen and who will help you.

Many have lived in places like Tent City, under train

stations in New York, under bridges, and abandoned buildings. When you're in poverty you're searching for a way to survive, and thrive at the same time.

There are various reasons you may have ended up in poverty.

- Mental illness
- Drug addiction
- Alcoholism
- Divorce
- Job Loss
- Natural Disasters
- Other people's choices
- Death of a family member
- Sickness & Disease
- Financial Choices
- Generational Poverty

There are different scenarios and events that occur, and fortunately when it happens, it can be the most devastating experience of someone's life.

The mind spirals downward, the emotions, feelings, and experience alone is humiliating, stressful, and worry, anxiety, and fears step into place.

2 CHAPTER

THE VICTIM

No one intends to find themselves in poverty. The one role many play when they hit poverty, is the victim role. Life isn't fair, and those in poverty may be very angry, bitter, and resentful. The stage of acknowledging you have been cheated out of life hits home.

The first one thing one has to face is the victim role isn't the way to survive in life. While there are many people that have played a role and did have a cause and effect on the situation, you also have to take full responsibility for your life, emotions, feelings, and actions.

Choices are made solely by you to participate in relationships, or hang out where you do in life, and with whom. This is not to blame, but understand the cause and effect of choices is separate from whether the experience was good or bad, or what someone else has chosen to do.

There are many times we choose to be in certain places and in relationships, and take part in things, we know is wrong, and we don't agree with in life. We have to learn to trust our intuition (gut feeling) and know what the best choice is for ourselves, and prevent ourselves from getting into certain situations, getting in bad relationships, and knowing when to act and refrain.

The word, "Victim" is a trigger word used in our society. The word may make you feel inadequate, insecure, and angry. The word makes you feel bad about yourself. And perhaps this is an important lesson to learn.

You're not a victim of your circumstances unless you choose to play the part. Life will throw many punches at you from different angles, and it's not a fair place. It's a competitive world, and there isn't always justice, and other times there is justice. Pain and suffering is a normal reaction to events, depression is a normal reaction to loss and grief.

While we may label people as depressed and a mental illness, the label feeds into playing the victim role.

Depression gives you a reason to feel bad about yourself, make up excuses, and the thought it must be true, this is my fate, becomes your mindset and belief system.

While Depression is a symptom of trauma and may

be a fact of life, the experience is relevant, but never allow it to define who you are, and never allow a label to define your future.

The root cause of your problems must be faced. Depression is more of an effect, rather than the cause of why you feel depressed. In society the word, "Victim" describes someone with depression.

This is why it is such a trigger word, it makes the person feel unworthy, useless, and angrier. No one ever intentionally finds themselves in depression or poverty.

Depression comes with a social stigma (mental illness). Western psychology sees what is wrong with you. Eastern psychology sees what is right with you. Both acknowledge that when one swings their thoughts and focus too much to the negative side, it can be very difficult to recover.

Depression is similar to an allergic reaction, to the way one is treated, and abused emotionally, mentally, spiritually, and physically. There are different types of depression, so not all will fit what I am trying to describe here.

Only a licensed psychologist/psychiatrist can diagnose you, and tell you what is best for you in your unique situation.

And we have to look at why people are depressed. In society 1 out of 10 people commit suicide, and 1 out 4 and 1 out of 6 people are labeled with some kind of depression.

This does have a big impact on our society. This is a lot of people. One question that comes to mind, why are there so many people depressed?

Depression is a belief system, and mindset.

Depression is from focusing on the past trauma and not letting go of the harm that has been caused. A fixed mindset.

Poverty is a belief system and mindset. The lack of materialism, the lack of money, the lack of love, and the lack of relationships.

By human nature we experience natural feelings and emotions in our situation. We are told by many it's not normal to cry, it's not normal to express ourselves, and many people don't understand how they found themselves in depression and poverty in the first place.

The first step you have to take is getting to the root

of why you think what you do, and what you can do
to figure out the root of why you feel the way you
do about yourself and the world.

3 CHAPTER

CHAOS & CONFUSION

Chaos and confusion is created by what we may allow into our life. One of the hardest things is coming to the realization that family has a huge impact on how one feels about themselves, how they see the world, and influences choices and decisions in life.

Some people are lucky enough to have healthy relationships. Others are not lucky enough and come from abusive families. Your foundation doesn't make you or break you. The family unit has had a cause and effect in both negative and positive ways.

We may live in one small corner of the world most of our lives. We may have never looked beyond that horizon. Society is another influence on your belief system and mindset.

We may attend a specific religion/spiritual community and they might have influenced you as well in the way you view family life, finances, and what they feel is acceptable and not acceptable. The world is a diversity of information, knowledge, belief systems, and mindsets. The world can be a chaotic and confusing place.

Your experience is taken in by your five senses. Sight, smell, sound, taste, and touch. Through those senses you have a negative or positive experience.

The road out of poverty is the Hero's Journey. The Hero that rides in to save the day is you. No one else is coming to save you.

No one is going to change the way you see the world, the way you think, or the choices you make. In retrospect, no one can save you from yourself. Watching the movie Ruffian, she was the most successful race horse, but she broke her leg.

The doctors, and owners tried to help her in every way, but she was caught in the illusion she was still running on the track. She ended up harming herself more in the end.

The point being, we can be stuck in an illusion, not see things, because we are living still in the past and not the present. Life has moved on, people have changed, and even though they may try to help us, the pain is still so great, we end up resisting the changes we need to make in our lives, and end up hurting ourselves more.

We may refuse to listen, resist change, take things personally, have a hard time accepting that what we may believe is wrong, and have the wrong knowledge, beliefs, or mindset to be healthy, whole, and complete.

You're the only one in control of your circumstances and situation. You're the author of your life. You're the one driving the vehicle down this road.

What you put into your mind does have a cause and effect on your emotions, feelings, and moods. Who you hang around does have a negative influence or positive influence on your mental, emotional, spiritual, and physical health.

What do you listen too? What do you read? What do you watch on media? Do you have a mentor, a counselor, therapist, life coach, spiritual teacher, minister, or someone positive in your life to help guide you on the path of success?

We live in a world that uses the art of seduction, a world that manipulates the emotions, feelings, and mood to sell you things through power of suggestion, or power of persuasion, and the world can be very materialistic and about money more than the value of relationships.

Chaos and confusion is caused by many people's motives, agenda's, intentions, and choosing to be harmful or harmless.

For some, ethics, morals, values, and respect for another human being is questionable.

Mixed messages come from family members, friends, society, religion, education, and the rest of the world. It's up to you to become a truth seeker and find your personal truth.

The Hero's Journey comes down to you discovering who you are in this world versus who the world tells you, you are as a person. The quest is learning to know thyself in and out and learning to trust yourself.

You are multi-dimensional person with layers of masks on, playing the part the world wants you to play.

Chaos and confusion begins from birth when we're told by our parents who to be in society, and society stepped in with religion, education, and the work force to help fill in the spaces, and friends, family, mentor's, teacher's, professor's, and other significant people added positive and negative feedback in our lives. We've become human conditioned.

There comes a time to stop for a minute and question those messages people gave you, what was successful, and not successful. What was their beliefs and what was your beliefs? What kind of mindset did they have? What exactly did they teach you in life? Were they a positive role model or a negative one? Were they abusive or non-abusive?

The past holds many keys to unlock the chaos and confusion. There are many successes and failures along the way. Unlearn what no longer serves your purpose, mission in life, and what you stand for.

While we may have liked them, loved them, and appreciated the part they played in our lives, there are just some times people that had very good intentions, but led us astray in their own thinking, mindset, and example.

At first it may be overwhelming, painful, and trigger anger. This is natural, and part of the process of healing.

We have to face the emotions, feelings, and acknowledge them, go through them, and release them. Letting go of the harm and forgiving is the only way to be free of the chaos, confusion, depression, and poverty.

4 CHAPTER

FEAR

Fear is your biggest obstacle in life. Fear will prevent you from reaching your goals. What kind of fears do you have? You have to push yourself through the fears.

Face them head on. Fear is always there, but you have to understand they are illusions. What's on the other side of fear?

Is it really as scary as you believe it may be? We get caught in the fear trap? There are millions of fears that pop up along the Hero's Journey. Once you overcome one fear, another one pop's up.

Tell fear thank you for arriving, acknowledge the fear, and let go of the fear. Anxiety, and stress comes with fear. The Jolly Green Giants we create can frighten us. We focus on all the negatives, and talk ourselves out of success.

We sabotage ourselves with fear. We rarely ever take the time to study fear, and move past through those fears. Fear is where we get stuck, paralyzed, and never move forward.

We gain fear from those around us. If they are fear-based and scared of the world, we have a tendency to take on their fears. If they've never been strong enough, or taken courage to get over their fears, they may influence us to do the same.

We can dwell on the news media, and listen to others tell us what to be afraid of, or decide for ourselves. Fear limits us from reaching our full potential. Fears says play it safe, and never get out of your comfort zone.

Today in society you have to get past your fears and out of your comfort zone to get anywhere in life. For introverts it can be very scary, they like to stay in the shadows and speak from a distance. Extroverts like to be on the front of the stage in the limelight.

Fear can be conquered, and we usually find out that fear is the only thing to fear, because in reality, fear is a big fat lie. Fear tells you, you can't graduate with a degree, start a business of your own, or have a successful relationship.

Fear is your best friend to help you make up every excuse you can why you can't break out of poverty. Fear loves to keep you in a limited frame of mind, and even in a small box.

Fear will tell you every reason why you shouldn't take a risk in life and become your best self. Fear will tell you that you will be alone, unloved, and others will judge you.

Fortunately, the journey is a lone one. While we interact with people you are alone inside of your thoughts. While we would love to never be gossiped about, judged, or have others stop telling lies about us, we have no control over this, and it will always be whether you are poor or rich.

Human nature loves to gossip and judge the next person. It usually stems from not being self-developed, understanding self, and dealing with their thoughts, actions, and behaviors. We follow the herd in the world, and the greatest people in the world are usually the ones that step out of their fears, face them, and learn to take responsibility for their thoughts, actions, and feelings.

If we hang out with fearful people, we become fearful of the same things. If we fear success we only have the illusion of fear to thank.

Fear leads to failure. "Failure" is another trigger word in our society. We get caught up on the fear of failure. Others project the fear of failure on us through stress, concern, and worry. The one thing you will find is others are to be sure to focus on the negatives of the world. Our society goes for the failure before the success. You will find Grammar Nazi's pick out all your mistakes.

You will find a reviewer bashing your message, because they have a different point of view and belief system. You will find the professor, critique your writing, and take a red ink pen and destroy your masterpiece.

Your parents and friends will keep a records of wrongs, remind you of them a hundred times, and bothered by you not acting appropriate in their definition of what is acceptable, normal, or healthy for them.

I suppose this happens everywhere in our lives. Failure is a major part of life. We failed many times as toddlers getting up on our legs, and learning to walk. We threw food around the room, and all over ourselves learning to eat. We broke things at times learning how to use them.

We failed at speaking our language, learning to read, learning to draw, learning to do whatever activity, hobby, or job we've ever had. We've failed at many things in life including relationships.

Through practice we became better and better at whatever we were focused on, applied ourselves, and took action.

Entrepreneurs and successful people see failure as a stepping stone, and don't dwell on failure. Rather they want to fail as fast as they can, make adjustments where needed, and problem solve.

Failure to others is a negative experience, where someone scold, reprimands, harms you for not living up to their expectations, and standards.

I suppose you have to know the difference, and stop beating yourself up, and getting stuck in fear, because some people deny that failure is necessary in life.

Separate yourself from what other people believe about fear and failure and see it as a lesson to be learned. Failure just shows you what isn't working. If it's not working make some changes in your life.

Figure out what the problem is, and fix it. Make the necessary repairs that are needed.

How can you repair your finances? Learn about finances, investing, and not just saving your money in the bank account. Find someone that is making investments and has the knowledge of what they're actually doing. We can follow the wrong people's advice when it comes to finances.

When you're learning to personally develop/self-develop the best counselor's, therapists, life coaches, are the ones that have walked the journey themselves.

There are many that have studied, write things, but never actually walked the journey. While their intentions may be good, I've heard many people say, they went to someone else, and found someone that had experienced it themselves.

Examples: Drug addiction clients may get help from someone that is an addiction counselor that has recovered themselves.

An anorexic might find a counselor that overcame anorexia.

A convict may find it more helpful to have a life coach that was in prison themselves at one point and changed their life around, educated themselves, and broke out of the streets.

While all counselors/therapists/life coaches/ ministers do their best to counsel, there are all different levels, and differences in theories. Western/Eastern philosophies and psychology can both be used and work in harmony.

Find what method and person works best for you. Take the time to investigate affirmations, positive quotes, success books, mental toughness books, spiritual books, psychology books, self-help books, and discover who you are and what you believe.

Learn about human nature, and how the brain works, the thought process works, and even learn communication skills. The more you understand the world and yourself, the easier it is to navigate your way.

Learn about healthy relationships, read books, blogs, study the differences between abusive and non-abusive relationships.

Never allow fear to stop you from achieving your goals. Find the truth for yourself. When someone imposes a belief on you, question it, and find the answer.

Look for the solution to a problem when it arises. Never wait for someone to teach you, and take action and learn. Take your personal power back and create the life you desire.

Poverty is temporary, not a life sentence. You have the rest of your life to become a creator, innovator, and learn to achieve success. Fear will only delay your progress, get you stuck, and at some point you will still have to move forward and take action.

5 CHAPTER

FINDINNG SELF-WORTH

Poverty steals the joy from your soul. Poverty magnifies how ugly the world really can be.

How unsympathetic and lack of empathy exists in our world. What people in poverty need most is an understanding ear, and empathic nature, and an encouraging mentor, teacher, or counselor to help guide one through the obstacles.

Most people that have been in poverty will say, once they've gotten out of poverty, they will never forget the way people looked at them, the words that were spoken to them, and the struggles they went through to get out of poverty.

Self-worth is a major key in leaving poverty. What the world thinks about you doesn't matter. What your family members, the people looking at you, speaking to you, and making negative remarks doesn't matter.

And I don't say that, because they're bad people, but we can focus too much on what other people believe and think about us, and get stuck. Our focus should be on taking action and producing results, and creating the life we desire.

When we focus on the audience, it's allowing them to take away personal power, distract you, and then fear surfaces, you get stuck, and delayed in your personal growth and success.

Self-worth is your major key to success in life. While you may love people, they are not wearing your shoes, walking through your situation, your circumstances, in your thoughts, memories, been abused, or traumatized in ways that you have in life.

They have no clue. And they project their world on to yours. Their experience was never the same as yours. Their experience is nothing like yours. Many people that are influencing your life have never reached self-actualization or transcendence.

Which means they are wallowing in their own pain and suffering, they have their triggers from their past experience, their issues they've never worked through, their personal fears, insecurities, inadequacies, worries, anxieties, and projecting their reality on to you from their own experience, knowledge, trial and error, and what they've learned.

Their mindset, personality, belief system, are completely different than yours. And while they may have their unique blue print in society, you do have one yourself.

We're all on the same journey regardless of social status, religious preference, ethnicity, culture, or society we live in at the moment.

You may measure your self-worth on what others tell you, what they project on to you from their experience, their perspective, and the reality they choose to create for themselves.

The world is filled with judges according to their personality, specific belief system, and what they feel is appropriate boundaries, behavior, and what is acceptable to them in their experience.

Your self-worth can never be defined by what others say. What they say may be relevant or irrelevant. It may be correct or wrong. What you say about others can be just as irrelevant, or correct or wrong in their experience.

Self-worth is how valuable you see yourself, not the way the world defines you should be, ought to be, and the way they would like you to be.

Self-worth is not based on how much money you have in your pocket, where you live, who your family is, or what job you have at the moment.

Some people value materialism and money more than relationships. Others value relationships more than money. These two values can clash in personalities.

Self-worth is loving who you are, respecting yourself, and finding pleasure and worth in who you choose to become every day.

6 CHAPTER

CAUSE & EFFECT

We all have a cause and effect on one another. We have to take a huge look at ourselves and how we interact and react in society. We can take things personally.

We can make it all about us when we're in arguments, fights, and debates with other people. Many people are in pain and suffering.

The anger and rage comes out when we deny our part and how we play out the role of persecutor, and judge in other people's lives. We don't like to be persecuted or judged. We do turn around and do the same to others.

We all have to take responsibility for our thoughts, actions, and words, and come to the realization we do have an impact on someone else's successes or failures.

We don't know what someone does behind the scenes. We draw conclusions, make assumptions, and allow our imaginations to create scenarios in our mind that may or may not be true.

We may think what is right for us is right for someone else. What is right for us doesn't make it right for them. What we may believe, may be incorrect or correct.

We are continuously growing, learning, developing, and everything is learned through trial and error as we go along the journey.

No one is perfect, and everyone is imperfect. Everyone faces the deceptions, lies, manipulation, and control of others influencing our lives. We do have a cause and effect on others, through what advice is given, and how accurate that information may be.

We have a natural tendency to want to protect others, hide things, keep things back, and deceive others into believing a lie, instead of the truth. Honesty is always the best policy. Everything hidden will be revealed, and truth always is found out in the end.

We have a cause and effect on the success of others. What is your motivation, intentions, and agenda? If you're angry, hurt, filled with resentment, and eager to pay back someone for the injury, the result is always a negative one.

We reap what we sew. What we put out there will we get back in return. There is no escaping the pain and suffering we inflict on others, and the responsibility we have in causing that pain and suffering.

We don't want to feel pain and suffering, but inflict it on others by judging them for their circumstances, their financial status, and their culture, their religion, their skin color, and their age.

We naturally want to fight back and get revenge, but if you notice, it's never worked for you, never brought you justice, and never relieved the pain and suffering inside yourself.

Usually it makes things more difficult, a bigger mess, and circumstances harder for you and others involved.

To a certain degree you can't control what other people are doing in your life, the choices they make, the words they speak, and the actions they take towards you.

Anger is natural, and the disappointment is deep. There is nothing you can do to stop the cause and effect one makes on your life or the impact it has on your life.

The damage can be huge, it can wreck your credit, create debt, force you to lose everything you own, and force you to lose your children, and even in some cases, someone may become a missing person, or killed by someone.

The pain and grief is tremendous, the wound is huge, and leaves a huge hole in your heart.

The burden is heavy, and never light. Life is complicated, a messy place, and unforgiving one at times. People have to take responsibility for the cause and effect they have on another person's life.

There are some things we'll never understand, or wrap our head around why people think the way they do, or why they have chosen to do the things they have.

We can only learn to forgive them, and let the pain and suffering go. Forgiveness releases us from holding on to the pain and suffering and carrying around the hurt and anger.

While justice may or may not be served, the healing only begins when we are ready to stop playing the victim, and let go of the offense. When we hang on to the offense, we carry around this baggage in every relationship we encounter, and the unresolved conflict inside bleeds out into relationships.

There are many people that have been through major traumatic events and have healed and are conscious of the cause and effect they have on other people, and there are those that have not healed, take vengeance, and want to make everyone pay for the injury.

It's a choice who you want to be and whether you want to cause more pain and suffering, and more destruction in the world.

7 CHAPTER

WHAT CAN YOU DO DIFFERENT

You've done things the same way over and over again throughout your life, and probably have ended up with the same result. When we do things the same way, we can end up going around in circles getting nowhere in life.

Who are the role models in your life? Are they walking the walk, or just talking the talk. Do they give out advice, but never follow the same advice? Are they a life longer learner? One that educates themselves, self-develops, willing to go the extra mile.

We have a tendency to hang out with the familiar, those who have abusive tendencies emotional, mental, spiritual, and physical. Those who have chosen the path of addiction, substance abuse, and alcoholism to cope with emotions, feelings, worries, and anxiety.

Those who have chosen to sit for hours playing video games year after year, gambling, watching pornography, and participating in unhealthy behaviors.

We can never have a healthy mind, spirit, and body when we choose to wallow in the bad habits and behaviors that hold us back from success.

It's not easy to break out of these habits, but habits that will hold one back from being successful in love relationships and financial successes.

These habits don't make someone bad or a horrible person. The habits just prevent them from reaching their full potential.

These habits are escape mechanisms to avoid pain and suffering. Avoid the negative side of human nature.

We can only go through life for so long, before we must face the conclusion that our thoughts, actions, and words, do have an impact on our success or failure in life.

Who we hang around is who we become. We pick up their way of thinking, we pick up their habits, and what is acceptable or not acceptable to them.

We do become what we believe we will become. When we have others influencing our situation and circumstances, the advice may and can be very wrong.

Take a good look at where you're hanging out, who you're hanging out with in life, and what do they believe? What are they doing to improve themselves? What is their strategy to reach success in love relationships and finances?

If you're hanging out with people that find it comfortable living off the welfare system, donations from churches, and taking advantage of the system, it's not a path of success.

While it may work for a period of time, it will not last forever.

If you're hanging out with people that have guns in their hip pocket, think they're big bad and tough, steal, and kill people every time they're angry, this is a lifestyle that leads to prison.

If you're hanging out with drug dealers, and alcoholics it is a dangerous place to be emotionally, mentally, spiritually, and physically. Stress, anger, resentment, bitterness, and victimhood resides in these corridors.

You have a choice who you hang out with, and

whether you participate. You have a choice to live in this lifestyle, or break out of it, and choose a better path.

8 CHAPTER

EDUCATION

The only way you will succeed in life today, is if you have an education.

Self-educate yourself and become an entrepreneur in writing, music, art, business, social, or spiritual avenues.

Educate yourself through a technical school, university, college, or some other training program.

Today in society you only get left back in the dust by not having skills to propel yourself in life.

The Meyers-Brigg's personality test can help you decide where your personality fits in a career search. There are open-source classes online, free classes from universities on You Tube such as Stanford, and Harvard University.

Google search is a good resource to find any answers about education you want to know.

Hang out in success forums like The Fastlane Millionaire forum, where you can learn to have a positive mindset and find a way out of poverty.

There is the Warrior Forum, and other entrepreneur forums to point the way to success, and give you emotional, mental, and physical support.

There's always a way out of your circumstances, situation, and honest ways to make a living. You don't have to take a path of criminal activity, or staying in poverty for a life time.

Personal Development/Self Development is another avenue to educate yourself. The more you understand yourself, the way you think, why you think what you do, and why you act the way you do, the easier it is to navigate your way through life.

If you're educated you can no longer make up excuses why you're in the same place you were five years ago, unless you deliberately choose to stay there.

9 CHAPTER

TAKE ACTION

Take Action and do something about your circumstances. Instead of feeling sorry for yourself, complaining about how unfair it all is, and worrying about what everyone else is saying and doing, take steps every day to reach your goals.

No matter how big or small, the adventure begins when you pick up your first book, when you take your first workshop, or attend your first class. It doesn't matter how long it takes for you to get there, as long as you are making the effort to get there every day.

Taking action is your number one key to success. If you're stuck and dwelling the past, the pain and suffering, the injury, and wanting to see revenge, you're not taking action to change your circumstances.

Others are taking action in the wrong ways, by judging, gossiping, rumormongering, and discouraging you from being a total success. If you're taking action, they have no control over where you're going in your life.
While they may have a negative mindset, most likely

they aren't taking the right actions in their life, and getting caught in the drama.

Take the right action and stay out of the drama. Let go of the struggle to prove them right or wrong. Let go of the fight. Allow them to believe what they do.

Allow them to be right for the moment, and continue on with your journey in life.

Words are weapons they use to break down your self-confidence, self-esteem, and instill in fear. If you want to take the right actions in life you have to believe in you. You have to motivate yourself. No one will be your Hero.

The majority will sit on the sidelines and judge you for every move you make.

Step out of their negative realm, and enter a more positive reality. Be self-reliant, self-dependent, and trust yourself. Understand you can make the right choices, mature, and become whatever you choose to become.

10 CHAPTER

VISUALIZATION

Life becomes beautiful once you're passionate about you. What do you want in life? Love who you were created to be.

Find a reason to become your best. Poverty is temporary, not a life sentence unless you choose that path. The personal power rests in your thoughts, feelings, and emotions.

What you think, feel, and emote, is what you experience in life. Visualization is a great technique to help you on your journey.

I'm not talking about vision boards. While many may use vison boards, and look at photographs, it doesn't propel you into action.

Visualization is seeing the person you want to be. What does it feel like to be there already? What does it feel like to be successful in love? Remember one person that loved you unconditionally.

What did that person do in your life? What did they teach you? What did they stand for? How did it make you feel when they spoke to you? What kind of actions did they take in your life? How did they express themselves?

What does it feel like to be successful in finances? Who modeled that vision in your life? What actions did they take? What did they teach you? How did they present themselves in body language, and when they spoke?

See yourself doing similar actions and similar words. Visualization is something that moves you into action.

See yourself with that certificate, degree, money in your hands, reading a book, taking a step forward, signing up for a class, attending classes, job searching, applying for a job, see yourself at the job interview and the conversation.

The more you see yourself doing, the more you will take action. Visualization is very simple, having a vison for your future. What is your mission statement? What is your life about?

What have you always wanted to do your whole life? What are your great ideas? What do you want to see happen in your life?

HATTIE SPIRITWEAVER

www.ingramcontent.com/pod-product-compliance
Lightning Source LLC
Chambersburg PA
CBHW070836290526
45795CB00002B/888